SOVEREIGNTY, STATEHOOD AND SELF-DETERMINATION IN INTERNATIONAL LAW

SPIRO PAÇO

CONTENTS

ABREVIATION

1   Introduction   Pg 7

2   Relevance   Pg 15

3   The Kosovo Case   Pg 17

4   Statehood   Pg 25

5   Self-Determination   Pg 28

6   Conclusions   Pg 39

7   References   Pg 43

    Appendix   Pg 53

ABREVIATION

EU	European Union
ICISS	International Commission on Intervention and State Sovereignty
ICJ	International Court of Justice
IL	International Law
IHR	International human Rights
IO	International Organization
KLA	Kosovo Liberation Army
NATO	North Atlantic Treaty Organization
Res.	Resolution
RC	Republic of China (Taiwan)
PRC	Peoples Republic of China
UK	United Kingdom
UN	United Nations
UNGA /GA	United Nation General Assembly
UNSC/SC	United Nations Security Council
US/ USA	United States of America

1 INTRODUCTION

The Kosovo case has been in the centre of all my works during my academic career. In this monograph I will use again Kosovo as the principal case but not in the light of the Humanitarian Intervention but focusing in three of the most important IL principles.

The self-proclamation of Kosovo's independence announced on February 17 invites us to some general considerations that may be linked to the specific event. [1]

The first is of a general nature. The independence of this country is inevitably linked to the principle of self-determination, universally recognized in numerous sources of international law, the Charter and in various UN documents. In concrete political history of the United Nations, this principle was explicitly linked to the right of the peoples of the third world countries to free themselves from colonial rule (or the so-called "UN trust") of European countries.[2] In this context, the principle of self-determination has been relatively easy to apply, as was evident, external and unjustified, a situation of foreign oppression. [3]

Subsequently, this principle has been invoked in other contexts and in particular in areas where intertwined and overlapping histories of peoples, cultures and religions: areas of high ethnic mix (with the predominance of one ethnic group of the oppression of another, as in the case of Kosóvo before 1999) and where the peoples opposing give reasons and have to claimed the rights to the same piece of land (not to mention only Balkans we can also get in evidence the Israeli-Palestinian conflict)[4]. The feature of this situation is that there is not a single legitimate interest, but a complexity of reasons and rights claimed which ideally should be reassembled in a

---

1 The full declaartion of Independence at : www.assembly-kosova.org/?cid=2,128,1635
2 McWhinney, Edward Self-Determination of Peoples and Plural-Ethnic States in Contemporary International Law: Failed States, Nation-Building and the Alternative, Federal Option (2007)
3 Sebastian Anstis, The Normative Bases of the Global Territorial Orde
4 Murray N. Rothbard, National Self-Determination

framework accepted by all. [5]

In the first case (that of the oppressed peoples from colonial domination) the application of the principle of self-determination was enough natural, in the second it is much more complex. In the first case it was simply to get rid of an external oppressor and, in the second case it was settled accounts with a neighbor or partner (perhaps authoritarian or oppressive)[6]. If it was the first to regain management of their own country - already legally formed, the boundaries established and internationally recognized - subject to the protection of "trusteeship" - in the second case it was often to form new states (disrupting or dividing existing ones), to change the boundaries and gain international recognition. [7]

Recently we deal almost exclusively with cases of independence and self-determination that applies to the contexts and model of multi-ethnic countries. Often we deal with cases as if they were related to the pattern of countries under colonial rule. So unfortunately it is not, and the roughness of international politics is such that, in obedience to reasons of realpolitik or more modestly aims of the day, they create the biggest debacles of the problems you want to solve: if you do not want to claim the "politics of two weights and two measures, "inevitably every wrong solution for a case is a precedent for another case, which - of course - will be treated in the same way (in my opinion wrong). [8]

This does not mean that you cannot accept or claim to self-determination and independence in contexts such as those of the model of multi-ethnic contexts. Indeed, in many cases it is necessary (the Palestinians have a right to their own state), but must be done taking into account certain rules that safeguard the rights of all.[9] The rules are basically four: the respect for human rights and international law, respect for minorities, the consensual (the opposite of unilateralism), the rejection of the use of violence (also contrary to the criterion of consent) to obtain the purpose. The cases of soft solution are rare, among them the separation between the Czech Republic and Slovakia. In the remaining cases has to do with situations much harder and not only for the obstinacy of the oppression of a people (or a scheme) to another, but for the perception of their rights that everyone has and that causes conflict expectations, interests and claims.[10] Alex Langer in a speech at a conference in Venice in 1994 (reproduced in

---

[5] Vansteenkiste, M. (2004). Self-determination theory and basic need satisfaction
[6] Antonio Cassese, (2007) Self-Determination of Peoples: A Legal Reappraisal
[7] Percy Lehning, (1998)Theories of Secession
[8] Wolfgang F., ed. The Self-Determination of Peoples: Community, Nation, and State in an Interdependent World
[9] Annalisa Zinn, (2007) Globalization and Self-Determination
[10] Harry Beran, "A Democratic Theory of Political Self-Determination for a New World Order"

the collection "Making Peace," Cierre editions, under the title "Europe's role in the Kosovo crisis") said: "It (Kosovo) is considered sacred by two peoples, Serbian and Albanian, and you know that the conflicts around the sacred lands are particularly intractable because it is the soul of their peoples and thus it happens that it is still more difficult than elsewhere glimpse a solution is not easy to say, but quite satisfactory. " [11]

In these contexts proceeding unilaterally, or blackmail of the use of violence, violate the rules of international law to achieve its goal (independence) is wrong and authorize others to do the same.[12] Creates obstruction in those who have to suffer the decision and power - even decades later - a sense of revenge and vengeance, of which the history of the Balkans is far too saturated. It will be said that international law must give way to human rights (though human rights are part of international law), but some rules are so criticized - in the name of humanitarian intervention - of international law, such as the inviolability of sovereignty and borders of a country, are established precisely to protect the right of self-determination and independence that would otherwise be continually challenged by the aggression of external countries. [13]

The people who want to self-determination claim the respect for human rights and these are constantly evoked by international policy to justify the legitimacy of their political and ethical positions and initiatives, even in the case of Kosovo. Beside the positive success of the promotion and evocation of human rights (and in Kosovo there has been a dramatic ethnic cleansing against the Albanians) in recent years there has been a manipulation: in their name, it was claimed a sort of "human rights imperialism" that hid geopolitical interests linked to political power and influence of certain countries.[14] In cases of international disputes and violations of international law only a "third party" (the UN, if it were more credible and authoritative) can claim the power to assess, decide and take action (humanitarian intervention) in the name of a principle of impartiality and universality. Anyone else (such as NATO and the US or EU), "can" but without trying to be impartial and universal. Indeed the today "Great Power" are often guided only by geopolitical interests. [15]

Every people have the right to self-determination to the extent that - especially in the context of multi-ethnic territories and federal states or

---

[11] Betty Miller Unterberger, Self-Determination, Encyclopedia of American Foreign Policy, 2002.
[12] Mary Ellen O'Connell. "The UN, NATO, and International Law after Kosovo." Human Rights Quarterly
[13] Independent International Commission on Kosovo. Kosovo Report. Oxford: Oxford University Press,
[14] J., Elliot A. (2001). War Over Kosovo: Politics and Strategy in a Global Age
[15] Mincheva & Gurr, Lyubov Grigorova, Ted Robert (2013). Crime-Terror Alliances and the State: Ethnonationalist and Islamist Challenges to Regional Security

confederations pre-existing - other rights are respected and the rules of international law: the right of minorities, all other human rights, and compliance with the consensus method and peacefully.[16] One has to ask if the self-determination should always be provided as a result of the formation of new states and not instead of other legal forms (autonomy, etc.).[17] For example, the leadership of the Kurds - who certainly did not suffer less than the people in Kosovars - does not require a new state, but a less ambitious recognition of autonomy within the existing state realities. In the ethnic drift the last twenty years, not only Kosovo, but a myriad of micro-entities have claimed the right to self-determination within the rupture of pre-existing state entities (other true, other artifacts, etc.) with the consequences of various types including wars and conflicts.[18] Among other things, the assimilation "self-determination = new state" (perhaps based on ethnicity) is a symptom of a weak and backward political culture, even inevitable in people who have been denied the freedom and identity. In this new era (that of globalization) the states should be overcome and should seek new legal and institutional roads, other than those of the nineteenth-century national statehood. [19]

In this context, the self-proclaimed independence of Kosovo - without detracting from the legitimate expectation of the Albanian people of that territory and the possibility of the final result of the independence - is today an obvious error as well as a violation of international law.[20] This because the rights of minorities (Serbs, Gorani, etc.) were not at all guaranteed in recent years (as also mentioned by authoritative international organizations).[21] Finally, because there was a fragrant violation of international law the sovereignty of an internationally recognized state and a UN resolution (the 1244, 1999, which recognized Kosovo as part of Serbia), never corrected or cancelled. [22]

Kosovo has never been given the status of a state, nor did it have the old Yugoslavia into the status of "Republic" (these were only: Croatia, Serbia, Montenegro, Macedonia, Slovenia) where only the Yugoslav federation granted the right of self-determination by the federation. He had a status of special autonomy as a province of Serbia, whose governments have since the eighties backed and then removed.[23] Even then compared to the old

---

[16] Antonio Cassese, ed., Self-Determination of Peoples: A Legal Reappraisal

[17] Hurst Hannum, Autonomy, Sovereignty, and Self-Determination: The Accommodation

[18] Marc Weller, Autonomy, Self Governance and Conflict Resolution (Kindle Edition), Taylor & Francis

[19] Crawford, James. The Creation of States in International Law. Oxford University Press,

[20] Raič, D. Statehood and the Law of Self-determination. Martinus Nijhoff Publishers,

[21] James H. Anderson and James Phillips , "The Kosovo Liberation Army and the Future"

[22] Text of Resolution, http://www.refworld.org/cgi-bin/texis/vtx/rwmain?docid=3b00f27216

[23] Glenn E. Curtis. "Political Innovation and the 1974 Constitution". Yugoslavia: A country

system of Yugoslavia (which was relied upon by the other republics to secede) this right for the province of Kosovo was not contemplated neither denied. The claims of Ibrahim Rugova - the leader of nonviolent Kosovo - have always aimed for enhanced autonomy for Kosovo as that of South Tyrol in Italy, in the course of his life he studied and visited several times.[24] It is invoked for the recognition of the self-independence of Kosovo the unusual paradigm of "'error cannot be postponed" and hence the need to hurry up in front of the obstruction of Serbia and the risk of a new wave of violence or Albanian rebellion if it was not recognized the new state. It is not clear why the same concern is not worth to other contexts, in other situations.[25] It is not clear why eight years after the end of the war of 1999 is too long a period for the Albanians of Kosovo and fifty years for the Palestinians[26] is a period not yet sufficient, or thirty years for Northern Ireland[27] (and even if we did vote them a referendum for self-determination) an appropriate period to arrive at an agreement. It was necessary to continue to treat and to seek interim solutions, such as those proposed by the UN on the Balkans and with focus on Kosovo as "part of Europe" (protected internationally and with a specific status), while supporting (as opposed to what has been done) the democratization of society and the Serbian policy, to create a fertile ground for the eventual self-determination of Kosovo. Deal, negotiate and still be treated.[28]

The solution of ethnic independence is acceptable. And it is the perfect example that of Kosovo. Even so, remember Langer, "the co-existence cannot be imposed" and, referring in this case to the Serbs, but his speech with great interest may be applied, at least in part, to the Albanian leaders: "I believe there are two ways to solutions ethnic clearly: one is forced inclusion of different ethnic groups, ie assimilation, denial of identity. (...) Forced bypass can go up to the expulsion from the ghetto to a larger tragic extermination "(also in" Europe's role in the Kosovo crisis. ").[29] This is not, fortunately, the case of the Serb minority, but this has been in recent years strongly discriminated against them and against Albanians still living in Serbian region bordering Kosovo. That, given the current situation, the mono-ethnic Kosovo is a state – the independence of witch – law the risk of conflicts in the region. [30]

The potential "domino" effect of the recognition of Kosovo is not known.

---

study

[24] Anthony Alcock. "The South Tyrol Autonomy. A Short Introduction"

[25] Thomas, Nigel (2006). The Yugoslav Wars (2): Bosnia, Kosovo And Macedonia 1992 – 2001. Osprey Publishing. Retrieved 12 June 2012.

[26] Gerson, Allan (1978). Israel, the West Bank and International Law.

[27] Robert Kee, The Green Flag: A History of Irish Nationalism

[28] James Ker-Lindsay (2009). Kosovo: The Path to Contested Statehood in the Balkans

[29] The referendum result at : http://www.sudd.ch/event.php?lang=en&id=ks011991

[30] The referendum result at: http://www.sudd.ch/event.php?lang=en&id=rs011998

It's a risk, not yet a reality. But it is clear that given the opportunity to some, this cannot be denied to others. In order not to repeat the example of the Kurds (this would be to revise the boundaries of four states), the Balkans, the Caucasus and - why not - Europe too "Western" offer many examples (adverse) of this type.[31]   And right there - close to Kosovo - Albanian minority in Macedonia (28% of the population) largely bordering Kosovo and Albania after the riots of 2000-2001 could return to claim the possibility of secession and not only federalism. And the same - topic overused by local nationalists - could make the Serb minority in Bosnia living in the Republika Srpska, ask for secession to. [32]

 Should not be neglected that the independence of Kosovo (like the war of 1999, and as the support to KLA) was strongly wanted by the United States: Europe, Russia and China accepted it considering the mas atrocities and need of intervention.[33] In this way it help the process of integration of the Balkans into Europe, but it feeds a fracture line in the old continent that feeds new tensions and new conflicts (in the Balkan countries the memory does not fail) and also a dangerous confrontation with Russia. [34]

The Albanian population of Kosovo has suffered a lot: it was trampled on, humiliated, oppressed. Their rights must be recognized, and its aspiration to self-determination cannot be questioned. The duty of the international community to support these aspirations and at the same time to take charge of the expectations and frustrations of other peoples and of the rules of international law and human rights principles.[35]   More than equidistant must be "equi-frendly" to all the parties that are involved in a conflict or a dispute. UN have to assert a right, not denying another, UN have to solve a problem, but without creating one more. Having encouraged the Balkanization of the Balkans, now the international policy must avoid the balkanization of political and ethics component of international law, and comity.

There have been debates on Sovereignty, Statehood and Self-determination among scholars for different case. Some of the most entreating are the case of the Republic of China (Taiwan), South Sudan independence and the question of West Sahara.[36] In all this case has been rise doubt on Statehood process, on the sovereignty of this state and their use of self-determination principle. The experience of this country's will

---

[31] Chechnya: The Case For Independence by Tony Wood

[32] Ohrid Framework Agreement Text in English :

http://www.ucd.ie/ibis/filestore/Ohrid%20Framework%20Agreement.pdf

[33] Krieger, Heike (2001). The Kosovo Conflict and International Law: An Analytical Documentation

[34] McCormack, Timothy, eds. Yearbook of International Humanitarian Law - 2003

[35] Beitz, Charles R. (2009). The idea of human rights.

[36] Shelley, Toby (2004). Endgame in the Western Sahara: What Future for Africa's Last Colony?.

help my in analysing the Kosovo case. [37]

The monograph will cover the three principles of IL and the examples of each of them and a paragon with Kosovo to understand if there are similarities and in if the Kosovo case has differences.

The statehood is very important in IL considering that is the process of state creation. Many are the examples of statehood in world history. Since the creation of the principle of sovereignty, after the religious war that and with the treaty of Westphalia, the creation of a state has evolved considering three basic conditions.[38] These conditions are the specific territory, a permanent population and a government that exercise power in this territory and over this population. The Montevideo Convention as a document basically of American continent states also include in the criteria for statehood the necessity to enter in to relation with other IL party.[39] The Montevideo Convention like we sad is not binding for non-member state but considering that is the only written document that list the statehood criteria will also be included in this monograph. [40]

The IL principle of Self-determination will be on the focus of this monograph too considering it as one of the way to archive the creation of new IL entity. Self-determination is a more recent principle then the others but its history, theory and practice is immense.[41] The origin of the term and idea also is in discussion and debating among historian and lawyer. The term have been used simultaneously in the same period (end of WW I) by the US President Wilson and the USSR Premier Lenin referring to the right of the non-self-governed territory like colony and occupied regions. [42]

Self-determination has its maximum application during the decolonisation process in Africa and Asia when using this IL principle the different native population archived independence. The principle was useful also in non-colonial situation like the dissolvent of USSR, Yugoslavia and the Czechoslovak Republic. [43]

Today the principle of self-determination is the legal base of many secessionist movements in the entire world. Only in Europe there are more than 50 regions or administrative territory that using self-determination asks for a full secession or internal secession asking for more right. Some of this movement ask for a form of devolution in country like the UK or Spain

---

[37] Makeham, John; Hsiau, A-chin, eds. (2005). Cultural, Ethnic, and Political Nationalism in Contemporary Taiwan:

[38] Steve Smith (eds.). The Globalization of World Politics: An Introduction to International Relations

[39] League of Nations Treaty Series, vol. 165, pp. 20-43.

[40] "Convention on Rights and Duties of States adopted by the Seventh International Conference of American States"

[41] Annalisa Zinn, Globalization and Self-Determination

[42] What Is Meant By The Self-Determination of Nations?".Marxists.org. Retrieved 2012-3-4.

[43] Innes, Abby (2001), Czechoslovakia: The Short Goodbye

and for regional self-determination in Italy or Russian federation. [44]

Kosovo is an interesting case that can be used to understand the vital interaction that this three IL principle have in the function of IL and International Community. This three principles can be considered the core of IL.

In many case Kosovo Republic is paragoned to case of secession like South Ossetia, Abkhazia or the Turkish Republic of Cyprus but this "States" haven't more then 2-3 international recognition. The Republic Kosovo not only accomplishes all statehood criteria but also have more than half of the UN member state that recognize its independence. [45]

Among the most important legal document that will be discussed and analysed in the monograph I can mention some that I consider the most important. One of these documents is the United Nations General Assembly Resolution 1514 on the Granting of Independence to Colonial country and People.[46] This document had a fundamental impact in the process of decolonisation and created the basis of self-determination practice but also other UN Res. Will be in our focus during this monograph work like the GA Res. Or the SC res. Another important document is the Montevideo Convention considering it the only written document on the criteria for statehood. [47]

---

[44] Jason Sorens, Secessionism: Identity, Interest, and Strategy

[45] Stephen, Michael, (2007) Cyprus: Two Nations in One Island

[46] United Nations General Assembly Resolution 1514 on the Granting of Independence to Colonial country and Peopleat : http://daccess-dds-ny.un.org/doc/RESOLUTION/GEN/NR0/152/88/IMG/NR015288.pdf?OpenElement

[47] "Convention on Rights and Duties of States adopted by the Seventh International Conference of American States"

2 RELEVANCE

A.   Description of Methodology

The methodology of this monograph will be e mix one. The initial part of any chapter will have a descriptive character that will focus on giving all relevant information that is the second part of every chapter will be analysed and comported. The monograph's analytic and comparative part will be the most important.

B.   Aim and Relevance

The aim of the monograph is analyse the process of statehood in the Kosovo case, its archiving of statehood by self-determination and the sovereignty of this new IL subject. The monogrpah will be concentrated in the theoretical aspect of these IL principles and in their application in the different case of history. To do this I will collect information from different case like the statehood of former eastern bloc state or the decolonization process in Africa and Asia and its consequences in IL actors.

The monograph also aim to give a precise chronological evolution of the sovereignty in the Kosovo region considering this a fundamental resource in understanding the problems of sovereignty and the use of self-determination by many actors of IL in this region.

This monograph theme is important because the investigation and research on the legitimacy of Kosovo independence and the road of legally archiving it thru a normal process of statehood that focus on the right of self-determination have been studied buy many scholar but now days the political and international relation criteria have overhead the legal one.

C.   Structure

Sovereignty, Statehood and Self-determination in the Kosovo case will be the main theme of this monograph. The big question is the accomplishment of the criteria (for Sovereignty, Statehood and Self-determination) from

Kosovo in its archiving of Independence using Self-determination.

The monograph will be divided in four chapters. In the first chapter I will explain the methodology use and the aim and relevance of the monograph. The second chapter will give a historical background of legal facts and documents that have influenced Sovereignty in Kosovo and will analyse the currently situation of Sovereignty conflict between Belgrade and Pristina. In this chapter will be discussed also the question of International recognition.

The third chapter will deal with the principle of Statehood, its criteria and the fulfilment of these criteria by Kosovo. In this chapter i will use many examples to show the flexibility of the Statehood criteria.

The fourth and last chapter will deal with the principle of Self-determination. Divided in four parts this chapter will give a historical background of Self-determination as IL principle and its theoretical and practice development. In the second part will deal with the legal basis and primary IL documents on Self-determination. The third part will give a detailed and description of forms of archiving Self-determination and the last part will focus on Kosovo Self-determination and its legality according to ICJ.

Is important to mention that the entire monograph will use an immense quantity of examples trying to give a full detailed idea not only of the theoretical aspect but also the practice development and achievement of Sovereignty and Statehood using Self-determination.

D.   Literature and resources

The literature and resources I used in this monograph are generally up to date books and IL journals but I also used some government sources.

One of the main sources was the book of James Crawford "The Creation of State in International Law" that not only help me with the theoretical aspect of the IL principles I am analysing but also have a great collection of examples on statehood and the principle of self-determination. This book didn't provide me much information about the Kosovo case because was published the year of Kosovo independence but all the previous process was well developed.

Another good source was the IL dictionary by Boleslaw Boczek that have a good description of sovereignty, statehood and self-determination that I use as guide in all the monograph work. In the explanatory and theoretical part of the monograph I used also the International Law book of Cambridge University Press.

A good part of my research I spend searching in online law journal. LexisNexis and Jstor where my search engine an I generally use only journal that I now as affordable. This thing limited my search results but made them more reliable. Most of them are university journals like that of Yale, Princeton, Harvard or even the Central European University Press of Budapest.

3 THE KOSOVO CASE
THE NATURE OF THIS SUI GENERIS CASE. THE SOVEREIGNTY.

A.   Historical background. History as Legal Basis.

In this Chapter I will analyses the different legal document, mainly treaties that have influenced the Sovereignty in the territory of Kosovo. The Chapter will be divided in different period in which the Sovereignty in Kosovo have been changed, contested or questioned, from the Balkan wars to the Declaration of Independence of Kosovo. The importance of this historical chronology is to understand the legal basis for or against the independence of Kosovo.

1.   The Balkan war, The Treaty of London (1913) and the
        Treaty of Bucharest (1913).

The Balkan war began in October 1912 between the Balkan League and The Ottoman Empire and finished in July 1913 with the sign of the Treaty of London and the Treaty of Bucharest. After defeating The Ottoman Empire the Balkan League had under its control all the possession of the Empire in Europe and the settlement of borders were leaved to the Great Powers. [48]
    In 1913 the Great Powers decided on the borders of the Balkan League with the Ottoman Empire and the borders between the Balkan League members. According to the Treaty of London (1913) the territory of Kosovo was divided between the Kingdom of Serbia and the Kingdom of Montenegro. This treaty transfers the Sovereignty over Kosovo from Ottoman Empire to the two Balkan states. [49]

---

[48] Ernst C. Helmreich, The diplomacy of the Balkan wars, 1912-1913 (1938)
[49] Handbook for the Diplomatic History of Europe, Asia, and Africa 1870-1914.
Washington, DC: National Board for Historical Service, Government Printing Office.
Anderson, Frank Marby

After some disagreement between the Balkan League, erupted the second Balkan war that see the Kingdom of Bulgaria in war with its precedent ally. The treaty of Bucharest (1913) amended the Treaty of London in some question like the borders of the Kingdom of Bulgaria with its neighbour but reconfirmed Serbian and Montenegrin sovereignty over Kosovo. [50]

Is important to mention that during the discussion over the borders the Kingdom of Serbia and the Kingdom of Montenegro justify their interest and territorial gain on Kosovo with economic and expansionistic reason without counting ethnic and religious differences with its inhabitants. [51]

2.   Versailles peace and the creation of the Kingdom of Serbian, Croats and Slovenes/Yugoslavia.

WWI brings new changes in European map. During the war the territory of Kosovo was invaded by Austro-Hungarian and Bulgarian Army. The sovereignty of Kosovo changed again in July 1917 with the Corfu Declaration and in October 1918 with its application that marge the Kingdom of Montenegro with the Kingdom of Serbia transferring their possession in Kosovo now in a single state. This document marks the annexation of Montenegro from Serbia. [52]

The union of the Kingdom of Montenegro and the Kingdom of Serbia is not the only change after WWI. In 1918 the Slave-speaking regions of Austria and Hungary join the Kingdom of Serbia and created the Kingdom of Serbian, Croats and Slovenes.[53] To this successor state the treaty of Versailles recognize, among others also the sovereignty over Kosovo, that didn't change after the creation of the Kingdom of Yugoslavia. [54]

3.   World War II, Axis partition of Yugoslavia and Communist Yugoslavia.

The German and Italian invasion of the Kingdom of Yugoslavia terminated

---

[50] Handbook for the Diplomatic History of Europe, Asia, and Africa 1870-1914. Washington, DC: National Board for Historical Service, Government Printing Office. Anderson, Frank Marby
[51] Report of the International Commission to Inquire into the Causes and Conduct of the Balkan War (1914)
[52] Dragoslav Jovanović, Yugoslav issue and Corfu declaration in 1917, Belgrade, 1967.
[53] Unification of Montenegro and Serbia (1918) - Podgorica's Assembly
[54] Ivo Banac: The National Question in Yugoslavia:Origins, History, Politics" published by Cornell University Press

with its division in new small puppet state like Croatia and Montenegro but the region of Kosovo was divided by the Kingdom of Bulgaria and Kingdom of Albania in that period in person union with the Kingdom of Italy. The armistice and surrender of Yugoslavia give to the victorious powers the ability to change its border but their legal powers and the validity of the peace treaty with Yugoslavia have been questioned. [55]

With the and of WWII the Sovereignty of Yugoslavia was restored in its ante bellum situation and Kosovo was created as an autonomous region of the Republic of Serbia in the Yugoslav federation. This is the first time that Kosovo have e defined geo-political position with borders (internal in Yugoslavia) and limited sovereignty (under Yugoslav sovereignty). The importance of this event will be in the fulfilment of statehood criteria like a defined territory.[56]

4. Breakup of Yugoslavia, UN resolution and Kosovo Declaration of Independence.

In June 1991 Slovenia and later Croatia secede from the Yugoslav federation giving start to what is known as Breakup of Yugoslavia. [57] The secession of Slovenia, Croatia and Macedonia and the rise of the nationalist sentiment and Serbian irredentism in Bosnia and Kosovo lead to a period of war and atrocities in Yugoslavia and created the situation for Kosovo independence. [58]

In July 1990 the Parliament of Kosovo elevated the Autonomous Region of Kosovo in the level of Republic inside the Yugoslav Federation and in this case also the power to secede from the federation like the other republics. In September 1991 Kosovo parliament voted the secession from Yugoslavia declaring independence of the Kosovo Republic. The Republic of Kosovo was recognized only by the Republic of Albania and had no control over the territory it claims to be sovereign. The secession was not accepted by Yugoslav authorities that invaded Kosovo and begin a policy of ethnic cleansing that obligated international community to intervene. [59]

From March to June 1999, NATO intervened by bombing Yugoslavia and obligated their trop to retire from Kosovo. In June 1999 the UNSC passed

---

[55] Jovanovich, Leo M. (1994). "The War in the Balkans in 1941". East European Quarterly
[56] Proclamation of Constitution of the Federative People's Republic of Yugoslavia, 31. 1. 1946. At: http://web.archive.org/web/*/http://www.arhiv.sv.gov.yu/a100008i.htm
[57] Glenny, Misha, "The Fall of Yugoslavia" (1996)
[58] Magas, Branka, The Destruction of Yugoslavia: Tracking the Break-up (1993)
[59] Statement of Albanian PM Sali Berisha during the recognition of the Republic of Kosovo, stating that this is based on an 1991 Albanian law, which recognized the Republic of Kosova at: www.keshilliministrave.al/index.php?fq=brenda&m=news&lid=7323&gj=gj2 (Albanian version)

the resolution 1244 that placed Kosovo under UN administration and theoretically without dividing it from Yugoslavia. [60]

The parliament of Kosovo declared the independence on 17 February 2008 and was soon recognized by many countries. Now (August 2013) its independence is recognized by 102 UN member state and by 23 out of 28 European Union member. Is important to mention that all Kosovo neighbor state have recognized its independence with the exception of Serbia. [61]

In October 2008 the UNGA required to the ICJ an advisory opinion on the legality of Kosovo independence according to IL. In July 2010 the ICJ rule that Kosovo Independence was not in violation to IL. [62]

    B.   Serbia Sovereignty VS Kosovo Sovereignty today.

Many political scientists have tried to give more precise definitions of the concept of the state, trying to enunciate the conditions necessary to ensure that it can be considered as such.

For Max Weber that State is to be understood as:

> "an undertaking institutional character of political environment in which the administrative apparatus successfully advancing a claim to monopoly of coercion of legitimate force in view of the implementation of the regulations. " [63]

Another definition is attempted by Charles Tilly:

> "An organization that controls the population that occupy a given territory is a state so far as:
> - differs from other organizations that operate on the same territory;
> - is autonomous;
> - is centralized;
> - its component parts are formally coordinate

---

[60] Text of Resolution at (English version) : http://daccess-dds-ny.un.org/doc/UNDOC/GEN/N99/172/89/PDF/N9917289.pdf?OpenElement
[61] Kosovo Foreign Affairs Office : http://www.mfa-ks.net/?page=1,4,574
[62] International Court of Justice. 2010-07-22. p. 4.
"Accordance with international law of the unilateral declaration of independence in respect of Kosovo" (PDF version of the Steatment).
[63] Daniel Warner (1991). An ethic of responsibility in international relations

with each other. " [64]

As we see in the above historical timeline for Kosovo the Sovereignty have changed many time in the last century. Now there are two countries that claim Sovereignty over the same territory and population. To determinate which of them have the sovereignty over Kosovo is not easy. Serbia argues that its Sovereignty over Kosovo was guarantee by the UNSC resolution 1244 and that the UN administration of Kosovo in post 1999 operated in Serbian sovereignty.

Hobbes:

> "The State is the unitary and sovereign instance of neutralization of the social and religious conflicts through the exercise of a summa potestas, expressed through the abstract form and universality of the law which is legitimate under the mandate of authorization of individuals, which realizes the mechanism of political representation; citizens are in fact in the pre-policy which is defined as the state of nature and the sovereign plays a "representative" uniting in itself the "dispersed multitude '" [65]

In the other hand Kosovo argue that using internal legislation (Yugoslav constitution) the elevation of Kosovo in 1990 to republic level by its legislative organ allowed the secession like in the case of the Yugoslav republic. Kosovo also use the IL principle of self-determination. The use of military force, the ethnic cleansing and the denial of fundamental human right are legal reason that allows the secession and self-determination. [66]

C. International recognition of Sovereignty

1. Recognition of Serbia as successor of Yugoslavia

The succession of States is a theory of international politics that concerns the acceptance by the other Member State of a just created state, based on

---

[64] Axtmann, Roland (2004). "The State of the State: The Model of the Modern State and Its Contemporary Transformations"
[65] Malcolm, Noel. (2007). Reason of State, Propaganda, and the Thirty Years' War: An Unknown Translation by Thomas Hobbes.
[66] Kosovo Autonomus Province constitution :
http://kushtetuta.independentkosova.com/english.htm

the historical relationship with the Predecessor State. The term can refer to the transfer of rights, obligations and / or owned by the Predecessor State to the Successor State, this theory has its roots in the diplomacy of the nineteenth century. [67]

The transfer of rights, obligations and property can include overseas property (embassies, cash reserves, works of art), participation in the Treaties of membership in international organizations, and debts. Often a state chooses whether to be or not to be regarded as the successor state of the entity that preceded him. The case is different if the Predecessor State was a party to human rights treaties, as the successor state should still comply with the terms of the treaty, whatever its policy. [68]

In an attempt to codify the rules of succession of States in 1978 was drafted to the Vienna Convention on Succession of States with respect to treaties. It entered into force on 6 November 1996. [69]

A recent example of succession occurred with the dissolution of the Union of Soviet Socialist Republics (USSR) in 1991. The Russian Federation was declared the successor state of the USSR and the Russia acquired the seat as a permanent member of the Security Council of the United Nations. [70]

In general, the theory is followed by the world community: a new government cannot be pleasing to others, but it must be recognized if it is exercising de facto control over all the territories of the predecessor state.

There are several examples in which the succession of States, as described above, was not fully followed. When the Democratic Kampuchea, Pol Pot's regime was militarily crushed by the People's Republic of Cambodia, backed by Vietnam, the seat at the UN continued to be occupied by Kampuchea for many years.[71] The State Taliban in Afghanistan has become the de facto government of most of the country in the mid-nineties, but the United Islamic Front for the Salvation of Afghanistan was still recognized by many countries, therefore retained the UN seat. [72] After four of the six constituent republics of the Socialist Federal Republic of Yugoslavia became separated in 1991 and in 1992, the remaining state, called the Federal Republic of Yugoslavia, claimed to be the legal successor, but was not recognized as such by the United States and, because of their influence,

---

[67] Buhler, Konrad G. (2001). State Succession and Membership in International Organizations

[68] European Journal of International Law – State Succession in Respect of Human Rights Treaties

[69] Vienna Convention on the Law of Treaties (1969) at:
http://untreaty.un.org/ilc/texts/instruments/english/conventions/1_1_1969.pdf

[70] Buhler, Konrad G. (2001). State Succession and Membership in International Organizations

[71] Ben Kiernan: The Pol Pot Regime: Race, Power, and Genocide in Cambodia under the Khmer Rouge, 1975–79 Yale University Press

[72] McGrath, Kevin (2011). Confronting Al-Qaeda

even by the United Nations, on the grounds that the Socialist Federal Republic of Yugoslavia was dissolved. The Federal Republic of Yugoslavia (later renamed Serbia and Montenegro) was admitted to the UN in 2000, and recently, in 2006, by referendum, Montenegro declared its independence and Serbia has inherited the seat.[73] The Republic of China was declared in 1949 as a successor state of the Republic of China (or Taiwan) and exercises sovereignty over China, although the Republic of China held the seat in the Security Council of the United Nations for many years. In 1971 she was admitted to the Security Council the People's Republic, in place of the Republic of China. [74]

The fundament of Serbian claim of Sovereignty over Kosovo consist in the fact that Serbia is the successor state of Serbia and Montenegro (1992-2006) that is the successor state of Yugoslavia (before 1992).[75] The IL concept of state succession give to the successor state the obligation and rights of the dissolved state. In this case Serbia considers Kosovo as a integral and indivisible part of its Sovereignty. [76]

2. Recognition of Kosovo Sovereignty by 100+ States

According to the website of the Foreign Ministry of Kosovo, their independence have been recognized by 104 UN State in the end of July 2013.[77] These numbers that can change in every moment are very important. We now that Kosovo cant be a UN member without not only a the needed majority of the GA but also the majority and non-veto of the SC permanent member.[78] But not being recognised as a state do not make you less a state. Some of the most important state of the world have problem of recognition, like PRC and RC that claim the representation of the people of China or Northern Cyprus that is recognise only by Turkey. The recognition is not a fundamental criterion for being a state. [79]

3. Recognition by International Organization of Kosovo Sovereignty.

The Republic of Kosovo since it declaration of independence not only have been recognised by many state but also join many international

---

[73] Sabrina P. Ramet. Serbia Since 1989: Politics and Society Under Milošević and After. University of Washington Press

[74] United Nations General Assembly Resolution 2758 session 26 Restoration of the lawful rights of the People's Republic of China in the United Nations page 1 on 25 October 1971

[75] Constitution of the Federal Republic of Yugoslavia (name later changed to Serbia and Montenegro) as new UN members.

[76] Participation of Former Yugoslav States in the United Nations". Max Planck Yearbook of United Nations Law. pp. 241–243.

[77] Kosovo government source: http://www.rks-gov.net/sq-AL/Pages/Fillimi.aspx

[78] Conditions to be member at http://www.un.org/

[79] Thomas D. Grant, The recognition of states: law and practice in debate and evolution

organization. Some of this IO the Central European Free Trade Agreement (CEFTA), the International Monetary Fund (IMF), the World Bank (WB), the Adriatic Charter or the NATO Partnership for Peace. The membership in all this IO can be considered as a real integration of Kosovo in international community.[80]

---

[80] Resource from Kosovo Foreign Ministry

4 STATEHOOD AND THE FULFILMENT OF CRITERIA IN THE CASE OF KOSOVO

"The State as a person of international law should possess the following qualifications:

(a) a permanent population; (b) a defined territory;

(c) government; and (d) capacity to enter into relations with the other States."

-Montevideo Covention Art.1[81]

In IL the concept of statehood has evolved during time and is more a question of practice and custom then a written list of criteria. The only document in IL that gives a precise list of criteria for statehood is the Montevideo Convention of the Right and Duties of State that consider four criteria to archive statehood. These criteria are the permanent population, a defined territory, a government and the capacity to interact with other states. [82]

The Convention of Montevideo is a document legally binding for its member states but it "is commonly accepted as reflecting, in general terms, the requirements of statehood at customary IL" [83]

> "The political existence of the state is independent of recognition by the other states. Even before recognition the state has the right to defend its integrity and independence, to provide for its conservation and prosperity, and consequently to organize itself as it sees fit, to legislate upon its interests, administer its services, and to define the jurisdiction and competence of its courts."
>
> - Montevideo Convention Art.3[84]

---

[81] Montevideo Convention Art.1
[82] Prologue of Montevideo Convention
http://www.tamilnation.org/selfdetermination/instruments/33montevideo.htm
[83] Montevideo Convention
[84] Montevideo Convention

A.   Permanent population

The criteria of population according to Oppenheim consist in the existence of an indefinite number of persons that live as a community though they may belong to different culture, race and creed or even colour.[85]

The criterion of population is not a question of number like it can look. State like Nauru or other pacific island-state has very small population but their being a state is not questioned by this fact. [86]

The Case of Kosovo meets the permanent population criteria considering that the population is not nomadic and no massive immigration or emigration have accrued. The ethnic composition is homogeneous considering that the Albanian nationality makeup nearly 90% of the entire population. [87] The Albanian population in Kosovo is a geographical continuation of the Albanian population in Balkans if calculated the Albanian population in the region (Albanians in south Montenegro, west Macedonia, north-west Greece and South Serbia) and have also a homogeneous religious creed. [88]

Kosovo have a population of nearly 2 million individuals and they are contested by Serbia and Kosovo. I believe that the fact that after the independence the majority of population have changed the Serbian passport with a Kosovo passport demonstrate their desire of appurtenance. Important is also the fact that many country that officially do not recognise the Republic of Kosovo have decided to recognise and accept its passport as legal and official. [89]

B.   Defined territory

For a State to exist is needed a territory where to exercise its power. The criteria of territory like the criteria of population are not a question of number but criteria of viability. [90]

The requirement of defined territory does not mean that a state with border delimitation problem is not anymore a state. Today many states have

---

[85] The Postcoloniality of International Law, Harvard International Law Journal, Volume 46, Number 2, Summer 2005

[86] "Republic of Nauru Permanent Mission to the United Nations". United Nations. Retrieved 10 May 2006.

[87] Rogel, Carole. Kosovo: Where It All Began. International Journal of Politics, Culture, and Society, Vol. 17, No. 1

[88] Bretton, Henry L. (1986). International relations in the nuclear age: one world, difficult to manage.

[89] Greek representative to Kosovo declaration on "Greece to recognizes Kosovo passports"

[90] I Brownlie, Principles of Public International Law (OUP 2008)

territorial disputes but their statehood have not been questioned. The case of P.R. China with Taiwan (R. China) or India and Pakistan over Kashmir are simple examples of territorial dispute that do not influence Statehood.[91]

Kosovo have been recognised as a geographical region since medieval time but its actual borders (with small changes) have been set during communist Yugoslavia. The borders of Kosovo during communist Yugoslavia have been internal borders of Serbian Republic but in the capacity of an autonomous region. [92]

C.   Government

The government is the most important and indispensable criteria for statehood. The criteria of government consist in a government that exercise its power over the specific population and territory of its state. [93] The forms of government are different. By this we understand that the form of government and the way it is selected do not interfere in the criteria of government in Statehood. There are different forms of government from the most common like Republic and Monarchy to government like Theocracy. In some state we can find even marge between the Republic and Monarchy like elective monarchy or republic with live term head of state. [94]

D.   Capacity to enter in relation with other states and International subject

Using as source of the criteria for statehood the Montevideo Convention we have to include the criteria of the capacity to enter in relation with other state and International subject. These criteria have been discussed by scholars and not all agree on its necessity but for the member states of the Montevideo Convention it is binding. [95]

The capacity to enter in relation is colligated to the recognition by other state of the statehood and sovereignty.

---

[91] United Nations General Assembly Resolution 2758 session 26 Restoration of the lawful rights of the People's Republic of China in the United Nations
[92] Benson, Leslie; Yugoslavia: a Concise History; Palgrave Macmillan, 2001
[93] Lauterpacht, Sir Hersch. Recognition in International Law
[94] Krader, Lawrence (1968). Formation of the State, in Foundations of Modern Anthropology Series
[95] Baylis, John, Steve Smith, and Patricia Owens. The Globalization of World Politics: An Introduction to International Relations (2011)

5 SELF-DETERMINATION AND THE CASE OF KOSOVO

A.   Historical background of Self-determination

1.   The Doctrine of Self-determination

> "National aspirations must be respected; people may now be dominated and governed only by their own consent. Self-determination is not a mere phrase; it is an imperative principle of action. . . . "
>
> - Woodrow Wilson 8 January 1918 [96]

The principle of self-determination was solemnly enunciated by Woodrow Wilson at the Versailles Treaty (1919) and was meant as a guideline for the tracing of the new borders, but in reality it was applied in a discontinuous and arbitrary, a factor that would have contributed not a little the gradual destabilization and subversion of the final of Versailles. [97]

In particular, the principle found application when determining the new borders of the power of the Triple Alliance defeated in the First World War.[98] There were organized plebiscites in Upper Silesia, East Prussia, in Schleswig, in the region of Eupen-Malmedy in Southern Carinthia and Sopron, with results often contested and subsequent source of international tension. Other areas, such as most of the Posen and West Prussia, the territory of Memel and the Alsace-Lorraine, however, were detached from Germany without consulting their populations, often majority-of the German language.[99] I passed the Sudetenland to Czechoslovakia together with Hungarian majority of southern Slovakia and South Tyrol became part

---

[96] Self-determination speech (11 February 1918) of President Wilson
[97] John Milton Cooper, Jr. Woodrow Wilson: A Biography (2009)
[98] Sally Marks, "The Myths of Reparations," Central European History
[99] Treaty of Versailles

of Italy despite being a German majority. The inner part of Istria became part of Italy although there was a Slavic majority. [100]

The principle of self-determination of peoples, it is fully developed in the second half of the last century, in 1945 at the end of the Second World War. In particular, it was the United Nations (UN) to promote development within the community of nations. [101]

The Doctrine of Self-determination today is a cardinal principle of IL and by the UN Charter it is binding to all its member state. The principle of Self-determination can be traced back to the Atlantic Charter of 1941and its eight points. [102]

The principle is not very clear in the form of obtaining Self-determination and the possible outcome of this decision. Self-determination can be used to get larger autonomy or full independence, to ask equal regional right in a federation or to be assimilated by a third party. [103]

The Charter of the United Nations, in fact, in Chapter I (dedicated to the purposes and principles of the Organization), Article 1, paragraph 2, identifies as the aim of the United Nations:"To develop friendly relations among nations based on respect for the principle of equal rights and self-determination of peoples ..."

Another major international convention that enshrines the right of self-determination of peoples is the International Covenant on Civil and Political Rights, signed in the UN in 1966. Italy has converted this Convention by Law 881 of 1977.

Another key step was the "Declaration on the friendly relations and cooperation between states" in 1970 in which decreed the prohibition of resort to any coercive measure liable to deprive peoples of their right to self-determination. [104]

Even more clearly expressed, the "Conference for Security and Cooperation in Europe" (CSCE), the Helsinki Final Act of 1975, which states the right of all peoples to freely determine, when and as they wish , their political regime without external interference, and to pursue as they wish their economic, social and cultural development. [105]

The content of the principle of self-determination consists of obligations for Member States of the international community not to prevent or hinder the self-determination of peoples, understood as freedom

---

[100] Treaty of Saint-Germain-en-Laye (1919) with Austria
[101] UN Trust territory list at UN Websit
[102] Borgwardt, Elizabeth (2007). A new deal for the world: America's vision for human rights
[103] Hurst Hannum, Autonomy, Sovereignty, and Self-Determination: The Accommodation of Conflicting Rights
[104] At UN online webpage : http://www.un-documents.net/a25r2625.htm
[105] Full text of the Final Act, 1975 Conference on Security and Co-operation in Europe
http://www1.umn.edu/humanrts/osce/basics/finact75.htm

of themselves to determine their own constitutional arrangements. [106]

In particular, the principle has been instrumental in supporting the decolonization, as it has enabled the states in developing hold free elections, give themselves a constitution of its own, choose the form of government, without any pressure from the more developed countries. [107]

In practice, it is in any case impossible to give retroactive effect to the principle of self-determination should enable it to call into question the territorial situations defined as a result of the most important events of the war of the last century, since it would put into question the certainty of national borders, the duty subjection of peoples and the political stability of states.[108] The Canadian Supreme Court, considering the claims of independence of Quebec than in Canada has carefully defined the limits of that principle: it is authorized to avail themselves former colonies, subject to military domination of foreign peoples and social groups where the national authorities refuse an effective right the political, economic, social and cultural. (Judgment 385/1996). [109]

2.   The use of Self-determination in the process of decolonization

On 14 December 1960 the UNGA adopted Resolution 1514 on the Granting of Independence to Colonial country and People as a legal link between Self-determination and the process of Decolonization.[110] This document with the issue of other UN Res. With similar content aim to create the new home-rule state in the colonial territory. [111]

Some of the most important result of self-determination in the decolonisation process is the creation transitional government like the UN Trust territory given in temporary administration to developed country with aim to create the local environment for self-determination and self-government. [112] Considering the difference between any case some colony get independence faster and some slower. The Italian colony of Libya gets independence very soon after the WWII considering the geographical and cultural vicinity to developed Europe.[113] The Colony of Somalia stays 10

---

[106] Allen Buchanan, Justice, Legitimacy, and Self-Determination: Moral Foundations for International Law

[107] Understanding Contemporary Africa, April A. Gordon

[108] Prokhovnik, Raia (2007). Sovereignties: contemporary theory and practice

[109] Full text of Supreme Court of Canada decision at LexUM :
http://scc.lexum.org/decisia-scc-csc/scc-csc/scc-csc/en/item/1643/index.do

[110] UN Res.1514 at UN website

[111] Birmingham, David (1995). The Decolonization of Africa

[112] Homepage of the UN Trusteeship Council at :
http://www.un.org/en/mainbodies/trusteeship/

[113] Vandewalle, Dirk J. (2006), A history of modern Libya, Cambridge University Press

years under Italian Trust government before getting independence and merging with British Somaliland. [114]

3.   The use of Self-determination in non-colonial cases

The principle of self-determination haven't been crated and haven't been use only in the colonial case but also with the aim to give a home-government to the many nationality and population that was grouped in diverse circumstance in big empires like the Ottoman Empire[115], Austro-Hungarian Empire[116] or the German Empire. From this nation in the end of WWI emerged many of the Central Europe state like Czechoslovakia, Poland Hungary and the south slave state of Yugoslavia. [117]

The principle of self-determination has been used in the above mentioned state also after the fall of communism. The peaceful division of Czechoslovak Republic[118] and the secession of the Baltic state (Latonia, Lithuania and Estonia). [119]

B.   The concept of Self-determination

1.   The Charter of the United Nations and UN resolution.

The UN Charter and the Universal Declaration of Human Right put the bases of a free world abolishing globally things like war or slavery but another fundamental document of human right can be considered the UNGA Res. 1514 on "Declaration on the Granting of Independence to Colonial Country and Peoples". This is the first legal and global document that affirmed self-determination as an IL principle. [120]

One of the aims of the UN was "to develop friendly relations among nations based on respect for the principle of equal right and self-determination of peoples"[121] The Charter use the term "people" and not "nation or state" considering the statehood as a right not only to form nation-state. [122]

The Article 55 of the Charter state that "peaceful and friendly relations among nations based on respect for the principle of self-determination are

---

[114] Trusteeship and Protectorate: The Road to Independence of Somalia at UNTC webpage

[115] Treaty of Sèvres with the Ottoman Empire

[116] Treaty of Saint-Germain-en-Laye (1919) with Austria

[117] Tucker, Spencer (2005). World War I: encyclopedia

[118] Innes, Abby (2001), Czechoslovakia: The Short Goodbye

[119] Beissinger, Mark R. (2009). "The intersection of Ethnic Nationalism and People Power Tactics in the Baltic States"

[120] UN Charter et UN Website

[121] UN Charter Art.1, para.2

[122] Discusion of the GA on the term State and Nation

to be developed" to encourage the use of self-determination. This Article is in full agreement with Art.1 of the Charter.[123]

An important part in the UN Charter have the Chapters XI,XII and XIII that deal with the non-self-governing territory and the trusteeship system created after WWII by the losing power colony. These chapters created the practice of self-determination in the process of decolonisation but no definition of self-determination can be found in the Charter. [124]

2.   The Decolonization declaration

Under the Declaration on decolonization "All peoples have the right to self-determinate; by virtue of that right they freely determine their political status and freely pursue their economic, social and cultural development"[125]

The declaration also calls for immediate "transfer all powers to the peoples of Trust and non-self-governing territories or all other territories which have not yet attained independence ... in accordance with their freely expressed will and desire" [126]

Decolonization formally lasted thirty years, since the end of WWII (1945) to the independence of the Portuguese colonies (1974). [127] However, during the 70s and 80s there were still many other declarations of independence, which went mostly unnoticed and that is not easily considered to be part of the process of decolonization. In many cases, these were the so-called "small piece of empires", which became microstates, who had no real independence and who came to be integrated into larger systems. There are three distinct areas that saw develop this phenomenon: the Caribbean, the Indian Ocean and the South Pacific. [128]

The rediscovery of Caribbean cultures, resulting in a resurgence of nationalist consciousness, led the former Dutch and British possessions in the Caribbean (Antilles and Guyane) to reclaim their independence.[129] The British possessions were more numerous, from Central America (Belize) to the south (Guyana): the first became independent in 1981 and the other in 1962. The following years saw several independence declarations: Barbados (1966), Bahamas (1973), Grenada (1974), Dominica (1978), Saint Lucia (1979) Saint Vincent (1980), Antigua and Barbuda (1981), Saint Kitts and

[123] UN Charter Art 55
[124] Declaration on the Granting of Independence of Colonial Countries and People, UNGA. Res.1514, UN
[125] Declaration on Decolonisation, UNGA. Res.1514, UN
[126] Declaration on Decolonisation, UNGA. Res.1514, UN, para V
[127] Corrado, Jacopo (2008). The Creole Elite and the Rise of Angolan Protonationalism: 1870-1920
[128] J.H.W. Verzijl. 1969. International Law in Historical Perspective
[129] John Connell. France's Overseas Frontier : Départements et territoires d'outre-mer Cambridge University Press, 2006

Nevis (1983). [130]

The possessions of the Indian Ocean saw their independence after 1968, when were decolonized the island of Mauritius and the Maldives, in 1975 it was the turn of the archipelago of the Comoros (excluding Mayotte) and the Seychelles in 1976. [131]

In Oceania, South Pacific today, had been subjected to European American and Japanese colonization. Britain made the first step in making independent Fiji and Tonga in 1975, Tuvalu (formerly Ellice Islands) in 1978, Kiribati (formerly the Gilbert Islands) and the Solomon Islands.[132] In 1980 it was abolished Franco-British condominium of the New Hebrides, resulting in Vanuatu. Australia became independent in 1968, the island Nauru and Papua New Guinea in 1975, while New Zealand proclaimed independent of Western Samoa in 1976. [133] France and the United States still retain today some of their possession in this region. [134]

The process of decolonization, however, cannot yet be considered completed. The UN, continues to report even a few dozen islands and territories remained under foreign sovereignty. In addition to the case of French DOM-TOM, and that of the Netherlands Antilles, Britain still does fly the Union Jack on a dozen employees were from the UK, including Bermuda, Anguilla, Gibraltar, Falkland Islands (Malvinas for Argentina), the islands of Georgia Among the South American possessions, in addition to those on the ground (which in 1959 saw the annexation of Hawaii as the fiftieth state of the union) and the status of Puerto Rico as a commonwealth of the US. [135]

3. The Declaration on International Law Principles

The UNGA in support of Res.1514 created the Res.1541, Res.2621 and the Res. 2625 that consist in the declaration of International Law Principles.[136]

The Declaration affirms the principle of self-determination as an inalienable right considering that "by virtue of the principle of …. Self-

---

[130] Canny, Nicholas (1998). The Origins of Empire, The Oxford History of the British Empire
[131] Lloyd, Trevor Owen (1996). The British Empire 1558–1995
[132] Macdonald, Barrie (1994). "Britain". In Howe, K.R.; Kiste, Robert C.; Lal, Brij V. Tides of history: the Pacific Islands in the twentieth century. University of Hawaii Press
[133] Fox, Gregory H. (2008). Humanitarian Occupation. Cambridge University Press
[134] Meti, Lauofo (2002). Samoa: The Making of the Constitution
[135] Cahill, Kevin (2010). Who Owns the World: The Surprising Truth About Every Piece of Land on the Planet. New York: Grand Central Publishing
[136] Programme of Action for the Full Implementation of the Declaration on the Granting of Independence to Colonial Countries and Peoples, G.A. Res. 2621, U.N. G.A.O.R., 25th Sess., Supp. No.28, at 10, U.N. Doc. A/8086 (1970).

determination of peoples enshrined in the Charter, all peoples have right freely to determinate, without external influence, their political status and to pursue their economic, social and cultural development" [137]

This entire legal environment created to facilitate the practice of Self-determination was backed by the absence of a clear definition of the terms like "peoples". Also the 1970 Declaration makes clear that "authorizing or encouraging any action which dismember ir impairs the territorial integrity or political unity of a sovereign and independent state will not be allowed."[138]

4. The instrument of International Human Rights

The International Human Right also gives importance to the right of self-determination as a basic right on the freedom of people to choose their government type and political belonging.[139]   One of the instruments of International Human Right is the R2P and the Humanitarian Intervention principle that also have been used in the Kosovo case. [140]

The principles of IHR being part of "jus cogens" are considered above principles like sovereignty making them the superior legal principles that exist. [141]

C. Self-determination and the forms of achievement

1. Secession by Constitution (domestic law)

The secession can be archived in Constitutional way. Many of the secession case in post-cold war era have been made by constitution provisions. The successful secession of the former Soviet Union Republic or the secession of some of the Yugoslav republic. [142]

The secession by constitution can be used in the case the constitution provide legal basis for secession. Some state constitution mentioned in the

---

[137] Declaration on Principles of International Law Concerning Friendly Relations and Co-operation Among States, G.A. Res. 2625, U.N. G.A.O.R., 25th Sess., Supp. No. 28, at 123, U.N. Doc. A/8028 (1970) [hereinafter International Law Principles Declaration].
[138] Declaration on Principles of International Law Concerning Friendly Relations and Co-operation Among States, G.A. Res. 2625, U.N. G.A.O.R., 25th Sess., Supp. No. 28, at 123, U.N. Doc. A/8028 (1970) [hereinafter International Law Principles Declaration].
[139] Morsink, Johannes (1999). The Universal Declaration of Human Rights: origins, drafting, and intention
[140] Hehir, Aidan; Cunliffe, Philip, ed. (2011), "Chapter 7, The responsibility to protect and international law"
[141] M. Cherif Bassiouni. (Autumn 1996) "International Crimes: 'Jus Cogens' and 'Obligatio Erga Omnes'." Law and Contemporary Problems
[142] Constitution of Yugoslavia and Soviet Union

first articles the fact that the state is Unitary and Indivisible giving the idea that secession is not allowed and other constitution like the Soviet one give the possibility for secession to all Republics that border with a foreign state or the sea. [143]

This domestic legalization of secession can be considered a peaceful and well now form for archiving secession. The constitution of Australia[144] and Canada[145] recognize the right of self-determination too but with some condition and with the obligation of a referendum.

2.   By compromise of the Parent State.

A well now form of secession is the secession by compromise of the parent state. Good example of secession by parent state compromise is the secession of Slovakia from Czechoslovak Republic. In all IL history this is the only case of peaceful and equal secession. Not only in this case we see the parent state supporting this secession but also the economic and political right of the parent state where divided in equal part between the successor states. [146]

In some case the parent state make an agreement on the secession of its province like the case of South Sudan that gets independence according to the agreement between Sudan and south Sudan rebel but only after some years and after the sue of a referendum. [147]

A type of self-determination by agreement and by parent state approval can be considered the Trust territory too. The case former Japanese islands in the Pacific under US Trust [148]or the Belgian Trust [149] over German colony. There are some cases the Trust territory had problem with the country they have been trusted like the case of Namibia trusted to South Africa. In that case the International community need to pressure South Africa government to give independence to Namibia. [150]

---

[143] Federalism and the Dictatorship of Power in Russia By Mikhail Stoliarov

[144] "Western Australia and Federation". Retrieved 2006-04-20.

[145] Rowley, Storer H. "Quebec Crisis Creates Talk About 4 Canadian Provinces Joining U.S.

[146] Paal Sigurd Hilde, "Slovak Nationalism and the Break-Up of Czechoslovakia."

[147] Southern Sudan Referendum Results website (SSRC and SSRB) http://southernsudan2011.com/

[148] United States Code: CHAPTER 14 - TRUST TERRITORY OF THE PACIFIC ISLANDS http://uscode.house.gov/docnotfound.xhtml?omitHeader=true

[149] Peter Langford, "The Rwandan Path to Genocide: The Genesis of the Capacity of the Rwandan Post-colonial State to Organise and Unleash a project of Extermination"

[150] Cedric Thornberry (2004). A Nation Is Born: The Inside Story of Namibia's Independence.

3.   Unilateral Secession.

The concept of unilateral secession in considered completely illegal and the right of seld-determination in this case is not recognised. In many case the unilateral secession can be considered as a foreign back attack to the sovereignty and integrity of an independent county. [151]

In world history we can find many case of unilateral secession. From the US to Belgium and Greece that in no possibility to get an agreement with their parent state declare unilaterally the independence.[152]   These secessions happened before we had a precise concept of self-determination but we can consider that some factors can allow secession in these cases. Factors like abuse by the parent state and mass atrocities or "broke of jus cogens principles" can justify a unilateral secession. [153]

D.   The secession of Kosovo and its legality according to ICJ. [154]

According to the International Court of Justice's unilateral declaration of independence by Kosovo on 17 February 2008 did not violate general international law.

The Court's reasoning is straightforward: not only the declarations of independence have never been prohibited by international law but by examining the context of the second half of the twentieth century, you can see how the concept of self-determination has evolved to become a real right to independence "*au bénéfice des des peuples territoires non autonomes et de ceux here étaient soumis à la subjugation, domination à la ou à l'exploitation étrangères*"[155], as well as by the exercise of this right that allow the emergence of new states. However, considering that some declarations of independence have also been received outside of this context, it must be inferred that there is no rule prohibiting unilateral declarations of independence.

Such a ban - according to the Court - could not be derived from the principle of territorial integrity of states, given that this principle (specifically recognized by the UN Charter) applies only to relations between States (prohibiting substantially that a state can attempt the integrity of another) and not to the people.

Nor - as called for by some members - the prohibition to declare independence unilaterally can be inferred from the previous cases in which the UN Security Council has condemned similar statements (and reference

---

[151] Prokhovnik, Raia (2008). Sovereignty: history and theory
[152] Finlay, George (1861). History of the Greek Revolution
[153] Fishman, J. S. "The London Conference of 1830,"
[154] Using Franch version of the ICJ
[155] Paragraph 79 of the opinion

is made to the cases of Northern Cyprus, of Rhodesia, South America and the Republic of Srpska,)[156] , since in these cases the illegality would be derived not from the unilateral character of the statement but the use of force or violation of mandatory rules of general international law (jus cogens). In this case, the Court concludes, the Security Council did not take similar measures and their condemnation of the exceptional nature of these resolutions would seem to confirm the non-existence of a general prohibition to declare independence unilaterally.

The Court of Justice considers that even the lex specialis, namely the Res. 1244 of the UN Security Council adopted on 10 June 1999 and subsequent Regulations of the UN Mission in Kosovo (UNMIK - UNMIK United Nations Interim Administration Mission in Kosovo) may be inferred a specific prohibition to declare independence.

This prohibition cannot be deduced in particular from the UNMIK Regulation no. 2001/9 with which it was adopted the Provisional Constitutional Framework of Kosovo since the purpose of that provision was to establish a legal regime of an exceptional and temporary non-final status . [157]

More and more: given that the declaration of independence would not have been taken by members of the Kosovo Assembly as an institution of provisional self-government (and, as such, it could only act within the limits set by the constitutional framework outlined by the regulations of UNMIK) but by members of the Assembly as representatives of the people, even the legitimacy of other exceptions are to fall.

In other words, despite the declaration of independence was taken during a meeting of the Assembly of Kosovo, the Court brings the declaration itself to a more general context, to believe that the authors of the declaration did not intend to act within the constitutional framework created by the United Nations (which would not have been able to do), but outside of it.

This distinction of roles by individuals who have signed the declaration of independence (members of the Assembly of Kosovo on one hand and representatives of the people on the other) is a novelty compared to what the General Assembly itself (which required a consultation of the Court, "rappelant que le 17 février 2008, les institutions provisoires d'administration du autonomous Kosovo ont déclaré l'indépendance du Kosovo de la Serbie") and it follows from a series of indices, such as the literal interpretation of some parts of the text (from which show a willingness to act outside the constitutional framework temporary), the absence pertaining to the statement, the expression "Assembly of Kosovo"

---

[156] Paragraph 81 of the opinion
[157] Paragraph 100 of the opinion

(only present in the text in Albanian, unlike the English text and French), also from the signing by the President of Kosovo, which is not a member of the Assembly , the different procedure than the one used for the adoption of legislative acts and so on.[158]

The legal arguments adduced in support of the legality of the declaration of independence appear to tell the truth: regardless of the ability of the indices mentioned by the Court to bring the declaration of independence outside the constitutional framework provided by temporary UNMIK regulation, it should be noted as the resolution no. 1244, however, impose a future political solution (which then had to take with the agreement of all the parties involved): political solution that in this case there was not.

---

[158] Paragraph 104 of the opinion

6 CONCLUSIONS

The secession of Kosovo from Serbia, solemnly proclaimed by the Parliamentary Assembly of Pristina February 17, puts the observer of international politics three problems. The first dilemma is legal, the second is historical and the third question is political-strategic. Given the complex diplomatic game played between the UN and the southern Balkans in the last nine years, should be made clear from the beginning the terms of the legal confrontation in place at this time, reserving the right to deepen the analysis at a later time on the historical and political controversy.

In contrast to those who superficially dismissed the decision as lawful because Kosovo supported by the majority of Western states, it should be clarified that, on the international legal declaration of independence is considered a relevant act on a purely historical circumstances in which, by itself, is not contrary to, and does not comply with international law.

The references to self-determination of the people of Kosovo, more advanced parts improperly, they have all the weight in this case. In fact, the principle of self-determination, as enshrined in Article. 1, par. 2, and Art. 55 and 56 of the UN Charter, the two UN Covenants of 1966, the Declaration of the General Assembly (AG) on the independence of the colonial peoples of 1960, from the friendly relations between States in 1970, by the opinions rendered by the International Court of Justice in the case of Namibia (1971) and Western Sahara (1975) and from its judgment in the case of East Timor (1995) and finally by the unanimity of doctrine, is configured as internal self-determination, and not external.

Has the right freely to determine its international status that people subjected to colonial domination or racist or whose territory is conquered and occupied by force, not that, then, what aims the establishment of an internal system of democratic type. It goes without saying that this type of claim, although, as we have seen, is based in legal terms, would have been justified in the time of the policy and regime of Slobodan Milosevic and the Federal Republic of Yugoslavia (FRY).

However, self-determination is in the principle of territorial integrity of states is an important exception, which is enshrined in par. 7 of the

Declaration of the GA in 1960. By virtue of this rule, self-determination must be coordinated with the historical and geographical ties of the territory than in the dominant state. Interpreted in this way, the principle of territorial integrity is a powerful brake to legal secessionist claims of a people. The Charter of Paris of 1990, drawn up in the OSCE and a significant tendency of international law to consider with today's growing awareness of the issue of internal self-determination to pronounce also do so. Even on a domestic case things do not change. The Russian Supreme Court, in cases of Tatarstan and Chechnya, he starred as the two principles just set out to deny the possibility of a unilateral secession from the Federation. Even the Supreme Court of Canada, in the case of Quebec, has denied that a province or a region, even when ethnically differentiated from the rest of the state, the right to secede outside of the three scenarios typical of the principle of self-determination of peoples.

Even in the absence of a right to secede, however, people, if it has the political strength or military, may also break away from a state. In other words, international law does not provide for the right to secede, but by no means does not recognize, based on the principle of effectiveness, the separation and the subsequent birth of a new state, as long as violated sovereignty and independent.

What has been clarified is true provided there is no help from third countries, which have the obligation to respect the territorial integrity of the state that suffered the secession. As noted by Professor Antonio Cassese, "if it is proved that this is the result of an autonomous action of the Kosovars, then there is no violation of international law." Obviously, the demonstration of the autonomous character of the action in Kosovo is largely moot in both directions and, essentially, concerned by the current diplomatic stalemate within the Security Council.

Based on these elements can then repel the fears of certain about the scope of the statehood of Kosovo proclaimed independent. In this sense, the practice of recognizing the nascent state by the UN preexisting we are seeing these days is legally constitutive of the international personality of the state to be recognized. In the literature, it is stated that the recognition of States is a political act, therefore discretionary, and not legal. Member States are free to recognize a pre-existing sovereign and independent state, as well as not to recognize, as the decision related to diplomatic considerations. The award, therefore, has no other meaning than an acknowledgment, historically, the existence of a State having such legally - that is, sovereign and independent - according to the evaluation put in place by the State recognition. And its usefulness is limited to the establishment of normal diplomatic relations between the two countries and, more generally, the various forms of which substantiates the life of international relations. It is no coincidence that the conclusions of the joint document approved by the Council of EU Foreign Ministers on 18 February entitled to leave to individual Member States to decide freely on the recognition of the state of Kosovo "in line with national practices and legal standards ".

Therefore assumed that the secession of Kosovo, considered in itself, is a fundamental legal internationally outside and apart from the scope of the principle of self-determination of peoples, but by virtue of the mere factual situation that has arisen, it is useful finally study the various legal interpretations provided by the parties involved in the crisis to the text-key to an assessment of the legality of secession from Serbia in Pristina, examples the resolution 1244 (1999) of the Security Council.

Resolution 1244 ordered the Government of the FRY at the completion of NATO air bombing of that year, to withdraw all federal military forces from the territory of Kosovo and to allow the initiation of an interim administration by the UN. The resolution postponed indefinitely the political solution to the crisis in this way. The argument given by most of the Member States of the European Union and the United States in this regard is that since the resolution provided for the dispatch of a mission "to ease international military and civilian a political process designed to determine the future international status of Kosovo "and because these principles were agreed, before the adoption of this resolution, by a meeting of Foreign Ministers of the G8 member states, this clause implicitly justify legally the final outcome - Pristina's independence - of this political process. In practice, the western states assert that independence is the result of a political process that characterizes the spirit of resolution 1244. In the same way they pronounce the document adopted by the EU to legitimize the EULEX mission, prepared under the ESDP.

The position of Serbia, the Russian Federation, China, and a minority of EU Member States (Greece, Spain, Cyprus, Slovakia, Bulgaria and Romania) which, however, abstaining in the vote, did not object the EU mission EULEX, consists of a categorical rejection of such an approach. These states argue that there is no resolution of the Security Council to authorize the secession of Kosovo. The reference argument is given by paragraph 10 of Resolution 1244 which expressly provides, and effectively unquestionably binding on the parties involved, the granting of Kosovo "substantial autonomy" within the then FRY. As this provision is unique among those of Resolution 1244 to rule on the status of Kosovo region, it follows that the assumption of independence is clearly excluded from the text. Moreover, with reference to the EULEX mission, governments in Belgrade and Moscow observe that the Resolution 1244 authorizes missions of international organizations in the territory of Kosovo provided that "under the auspices of the UN," element which would hence lacking the EU mission.

The position advanced by western states is very weak. The proof is given by the fact that the joint document adopted under the ESDP and the EU on the EULEX mission, after justifying the final outcome of the political process called Resolution 1244, however, is quick to recognize that the references of the Preamble to Kosovo as an integral part of the territory of the FRY and the respect of the principle of territorial integrity of the FRY are not binding. Famously, the clauses in the initial part of the resolutions of the Security Council are not in fact binding, as opposed to text device, even in cases where these are adopted Chapter VII of the UN Charter. But it turns out the least, paradoxical and ultimately to reject the position of Western states the argument that what is expressly stated in the operative part of the resolution - the territorial integrity of the FRY and the status of mere autonomy of Kosovo - should not be considered binding, while what was agreed in a multilateral political forum devoid of binding powers and alien to the Security Council, which is the G8, and that is not unequivocally enshrined in the resolution - that is to say that the final outcome of the political process could provide for the independence of the Kosovo - appears instead binding, even if only implicitly.

In the light of this analysis I conclude that the Sovereignty and Statehood of Kosovo in the focus of self-determination is and will remain a siu generis case considering all the above reflection.

REFERENCES

The full declaration of Independence of Kosovo

McWhinney, Edward
"Self-Determination of Peoples and Plural-Ethnic States in Contemporary
International Law : Failed States, Nation-Building and the Alternative"

Sebastian Anstis,
The Normative Bases of the Global Territorial Orde

Murray N. Rothbard,
National Self-Determination

Vansteenkiste, M. (2004).
Self-determination theory and basic need satisfaction

Antonio Cassese, (2007)
Self-Determination of Peoples: A Legal Reappraisal

Percy Lehning, (1998)
Theories of Secession

Wolfgang F.,
The Self-Determination of Peoples: Community, Nation, and State in an
Interdependent World

Annalisa Zinn, (2007)
Globalization and Self-Determination

Harry Beran,
"A Democratic Theory of Political Self-Determination for a New World
Order"

Betty Miller Unterberger,
Self-Determination, Encyclopedia of American Foreign Policy, 2002.

Mary Ellen O'Connell.
"The UN, NATO, and International Law after Kosovo." Human Rights
Quarterly

Independent International Commission on Kosovo. Kosovo Report.
Oxford: Oxford University Press,

J., Elliot A. (2001).
War Over Kosovo: Politics and Strategy in a Global Age

Mincheva & Gurr, Lyubov Grigorova, Ted Robert (2013).
Crime-Terror Alliances and the State: Ethnonationalist and Islamist
Challenges to Regional Security

Antonio Cassese,
Self-Determination of Peoples: A Legal Reappraisal

Hurst Hannum,
Autonomy, Sovereignty, and Self-Determination: The Accommodation of
Conflicting Rights, University of Pennsylvania Press, 1996.

Marc Weller,
Autonomy, Self Governance and Conflict Resolution (Kindle Edition),
Taylor & Francis

Crawford, James.
The Creation of States in International Law. Oxford University Press, 2005.

Rai, D.
Statehood and the Law of Self-determination. Martinus Nijhoff Publishers,
2002.

James H. Anderson and James Phillips ,
"The Kosovo Liberation Army and the Future of Kosovo"

Glenn E. Curtis.
"Political Innovation and the 1974 Constitution". Yugoslavia: A country
study

Anthony Alcock.
"The South Tyrol Autonomy. A Short Introduction"

Thomas, Nigel (2006).
The Yugoslav Wars (2): Bosnia, Kosovo And Macedonia 1992 - 2001.
Osprey Publishing. Retrieved 12 June 2012.

Gerson, Allan (1978).
Israel, the West Bank and International Law.

Robert Kee,
The Green Flag: A History of Irish Nationalism

James Ker-Lindsay (2009).
Kosovo: The Path to Contested Statehood in the Balkans

Tony Wood
Chechnya: The Case For Independence

Ohrid Framework Agreement Text

Krieger, Heike (2001).
The Kosovo Conflict and International Law: An Analytical Documentation

McCormack, Timothy,
Yearbook of International Humanitarian Law – 2003

Beitz, Charles R. (2009).
The idea of human rights.

Shelley, Toby (2004).
Endgame in the Western Sahara: What Future for Africa's Last Colony?.

Makeham, John; Hsiau, A-chin, (2005).
Cultural, Ethnic, and Political Nationalism in Contemporary Taiwan

Steve Smith
The Globalization of World Politics: An Introduction to International Relations

League of Nations Treaty Series

"Convention on Rights and Duties of States adopted by the Seventh

LL.M. Spiro Paço

International Conference of American States"

Annalisa Zinn,
Globalization and Self-Determination

What Is Meant By The Self-Determination of Nations?". Marxists.org.
Retrieved 2012-03-04.

Innes, Abby (2001),
Czechoslovakia: The Short Goodbye

Jason Sorens,
Secessionism: Identity, Interest, and Strategy

Stephen, Michael, (2007)
Cyprus: Two Nations in One Island

"Convention on Rights and Duties of States adopted by the Seventh
International Conference of American States"

Ernst C. Helmreich,
The diplomacy of the Balkan wars, 1912-1913 (1938)

Anderson, Frank Marby
Handbook for the Diplomatic History of Europe, Asia, and Africa 1870-
1914. Washington, DC: National Board for Historical Service, Government
Printing Office.

Report of the International Commission to Inquire into the Causes and
Conduct of the Balkan War (1914)

The Corfu Declaration

Unification of Montenegro and Serbia (1918) - Podgorica's Assembly

Ivo Banac:
The National Question in Yugoslavia:Origins, History, Politics" published
by Cornell University Press

Jovanovich, Leo M. (1994).

"The War in the Balkans in 1941". East European Quarterly

Proclamation of Constitution of the Federative People's Republic of
Yugoslavia, 31. 1. 1946. At:

Glenny, Misha,
"The Fall of Yugoslavia" (1996)

Magas, Branka,
The Destruction of Yugoslavia: Tracking the Break-up (1993)

Daniel Warner (1991).
An ethic of responsibility in international relations

Axtmann, Roland (2004).
"The State of the State: The Model of the Modern State and Its
Contemporary Transformations"

Malcolm, Noel. (2007).
Reason of State, Propaganda, and the Thirty Years' War: An Unknown
Translation by Thomas Hobbes.

Kosovo Autonomus Province constitution

Buhler, Konrad G. (2001).
State Succession and Membership in International Organizations European
Journal of International Law State Succession in Respect of Human Rights
Treaties Vienna Convention on the Law of Treaties (1969)

Buhler, Konrad G. (2001).
State Succession and Membership in International Organizations

Ben Kiernan:
The Pol Pot Regime: Race, Power, and Genocide in Cambodia under the
Khmer Rouge,

McGrath, Kevin (2011).
Confronting Al-Qaeda

Sabrina P. Ramet.
Serbia Since 1989: Politics and Society Under Milosevic and After.
University of Washington Press

United Nations General Assembly Resolution 2758 session 26 Restoration of the lawful rights of the People's Republic of China in the United Nations page 1 on 25 October 1971

Macedonia, and the Federal Republic of Yugoslavia (name later changed to Serbia and Montenegro) as new UN members.

Participation of Former Yugoslav States in the United Nations". Max Planck Yearbook of United Nations Law. pp. 241–243.

Thomas D. Grant,
The recognition of states: law and practice in debate and evolution Montevideo Convention

The Postcoloniality of International Law, Harvard International Law Journal, Volume 46, Number 2, Summer 2005

"Republic of Nauru Permanent Mission to the United Nations". United Nations. Retrieved 10 May 2006.

Rogel, Carole.
Kosovo: Where It All Began. International Journal of Politics, Culture, and Society,

Bretton, Henry L. (1986).
International relations in the nuclear age: one world, difficult to manage

Greek representative to Kosovo declaration on "Greece to recognizes Kosovo passports"

I Brownlie,
Principles of Public International Law (OUP 2008)

United Nations General Assembly Resolution 2758 session 26 Restoration of the lawful rights of the People's Republic of China in the United Nations

Benson, Leslie;
Yugoslavia: a Concise History; Palgrave Macmillan, 2001

Lauterpacht, Sir Hersch.
Recognition in International Law

Krader, Lawrence (1968).

Formation of the State, in Foundations of Modern Anthropology Series

Baylis, John, Steve Smith, and Patricia Owens.
The Globalization of World Politics: An Introduction to International Relations (2011)

Self-determination speech (11 February 1918) of President Wilson

John Milton Cooper, Jr. Woodrow Wilson:
A Biography (2009)

Sally Marks,
"The Myths of Reparations," Central European History

Treaty of Versailles

Treaty of Saint-Germain-en-Laye (1919) with Austria

Borgwardt, Elizabeth (2007).
A new deal for the world: America's vision for human rights

Hurst Hannum, Autonomy,
Sovereignty, and Self-Determination: The Accommodation of Conflicting Rights

At UN online webpage : http://www.un-documents.net/a25r2625.htm

Full text of the Final Act, 1975 Conference on Security and Co-operation in Europe

Allen Buchanan,
Justice, Legitimacy, and Self-Determination: Moral Foundations for International Law

Understanding Contemporary Africa, April A. Gordon

Prokhovnik, Raia (2007).
Sovereignties: contemporary theory and practice

Full text of Supreme Court of Canada decision ON Quebec secession:

Birmingham, David (1995).
The Decolonization of Africa

Vandewalle, Dirk J. (2006),
A history of modern Libya, Cambridge University Press

Trusteeship and Protectorate: The Road to Independence of Somalia at
UNTC webpage

Treaty of Sevres with the Ottoman Empire

Treaty of Saint-Germain-en-Laye (1919) with Austria

Tucker, Spencer (2005).
World War I: encyclopedia

Innes, Abby (2001),
Czechoslovakia: The Short Goodbye

Beissinger, Mark R. (2009).
"The intersection of Ethnic Nationalism and People Power Tactics in the
Baltic States"

Declaration on the Granting of Independence of Colonial Countries and
People, UNGA. Res.1514, UN

Declaration on Decolonisation, UNGA. Res.1514, UN

Corrado, Jacopo (2008).
The Creole Elite and the Rise of Angolan Protonationalism: 1870-1920

J.H.W. Verzijl. 1969.
International Law in Historical Perspective

John Connell.
France's Overseas Frontier : Départements et territoires d'outre-mer
Cambridge University Press, 2006

Canny, Nicholas (1998).
The Origins of Empire, The Oxford History of the British Empire

Lloyd, Trevor Owen (1996).
The British Empire 1558–1995
Macdonald, Barrie (1994).
"Britain". In Howe, K.R.; Kiste, Robert C.; Lal, Brij V. Tides of history: the

Pacific Islands in the twentieth century. University of Hawaii Press

Fox, Gregory H. (2008).
Humanitarian Occupation. Cambridge University Press

Meti, Lauofo (2002).
Samoa: The Making of the Constitution

Cahill, Kevin (2010).
Who Owns the World: The Surprising Truth About Every Piece of Land
on the

Programme of Action for the Full Implementation of the Declaration on
the Granting of Independence to Colonial Countries and Peoples

Declaration on Principles of International Law Concerning Friendly
Relations and Co-operationAmong States

Morsink, Johannes (1999).
The Universal Declaration of Human Rights: origins, drafting, and intention

M. Cherif Bassiouni. (Autumn 1996)
"International Crimes: 'Jus Cogens' and 'Obligatio

Erga Omnes'.
" Law and Contemporary Problems

Constitution of Yugoslavia and Soviet Union

Mikhail Stoliarov
Federalism and the Dictatorship of Power in Russia

"Western Australia and Federation". Retrieved 2006-04-20.

Rowley, Storer H.
"Quebec Crisis Creates Talk About 4 Canadian Provinces Joining U.S.

Paal Sigurd Hilde,
"Slovak Nationalism and the Break-Up of Czechoslovakia."

Southern Sudan Referendum Results

United States Code: CHAPTER 14 - TRUST TERRITORY OF THE

PACIFIC ISLANDS

Peter Langford,
"The Rwandan Path to Genocide: The Genesis of the Capacity of the
Rwandan Post-colonial State to Organise and Unleash a project of
Extermination"

Cedric Thornberry (2004).
A Nation Is Born: The Inside Story of Namibia's Independence.

Prokhovnik, Raia (2008).
Sovereignty: history and theory

Finlay, George (1861).
History of the Greek Revolution

Fishman, J. S.
"The London Conference of 1830,"

ICJ advisory opinion on the Kosovo declaration of independence

APPENDIX

UN Member state Recognition of Kosovo Independence
(February 2014)

1	Afghanistan	18 February 2008
2	Costa Rica	18 February 2008
3	Albania	18 February 2008
4	France	18 February 2008
5	Senegal	18 February 2008
6	Turkey	18 February 2008
7	UK	18 February 2008
8	United States	18 February 2008
9	Australia	19 February 2008
10	Latvia	20 February 2008
11	Germany	20 February 2008
12	Estonia	21 February 2008
13	Italy	21 February 2008
14	Denmark	21 February 2008
15	Luxembourg	21 February 2008
16	Peru	22 February 2008
17	Belgium	24 February 2008
18	Poland	26 February 2008
19	Switzerland	27 February 2008
20	Austria	28 February 2008
21	Ireland	29 February 2008
22	Sweden	4 March 2008
23	Netherlands	4 March 2008
24	Iceland	5 March 2008
25	Slovenia	5 March 2008
26	Finland	7 March 2008
27	Japan	18 March 2008
28	Canada	18 March 2008

29	Monaco	19 March 2008
30	Hungary	19 March 2008
31	Croatia	19 March 2008
32	Bulgaria	20 March 2008
33	Liechtenstein	25 March 2008
34	South Korea	28 March 2008
35	Norway	28 March 2008
36	M. Islands	17 April 2008
37	Burkina Faso	23 April 2008
38	Nauru	23 April 2008
39	Lithuania	6 May 2008
40	San Marino	12 May 2008
41	Czech Rep.	21 May 2008
42	Liberia	30 May 2008
43	Sierra Leone	11 June 2008
44	Colombia	4 August 2008
45	Belize	7 August 2008
46	Malta	22 August 2008
47	Samoa	15 Sep 2008
48	Portugal	7 October 2008
49	Montenegro	9 October 2008
50	Macedonia	9 October 2008
51	UAE	14 October 2008
52	Malaysia	30 October 2008
53	FSM	5 December 2008
54	Panama	16 January 2009
55	Maldives	19 February 2009
56	Palau	6 March 2009
57	Gambia	7 April 2009
58	Saudi Arabia	20 April 2009
59	Comoros	14 May 2009
60	Bahrain	19 May 2009
61	Jordan	7 July 2009
62	Dom. Rep.	10 July 2009
63	New Zealan	9 November 2009
64	Malawi	14 Dec 2009
65	Mauritania	12 January 2010
66	Swaziland	12 April 2010
67	Vanuatu	28 April 2010
68	Djibouti	8 May 2010
69	Somalia	19 May 2010
70	Honduras	3 September 2010
71	Kiribati	21 October 2010

72	Tuvalu	18 Nov 2010
73	Qatar	7 January 2011
74	Guinea-Biss.	10 January 2011
75	Oman	4 February 2011
76	Andorra	8 June 2011
77	CAR	22 July 2011
78	Guinea	12 August 2011
79	Niger	15 August 2011
80	Benin	18 August 2011
81	Saint Lucia	19 August 2011
82	Gabon	15 Sep 2011
83	Ivory Coast	16 Sep 2011
84	Kuwait	11 October 2011
85	Uganda	5 December 2011
86	Ghana	23 January 2012
87	Haiti	10 February 2012
88	STP	13 March 2012
89	Brunei	25 April 2012
90	Chad	1 June 2012
91	Timor-Leste	20 Sep 2012
92	PNG	3 October 2012
93	Burundi	16 October 2012
94	Fiji	19 Nov 2012
95	St. Kitts Nevis	28 Nov 2012
96	Dominica	11 Dec 2012
97	Pakistan	24 Dec 2012
98	Guyana	16 March 2013
99	Tanzania	29 May 2013
100	Yemen	11 June 2013
101	Egypt	26 June 2013
102	El Salvador	29 June 2013
103	Thailand	24 Sep 2013
104	Grenada	25 Sep 2013
105	Libya	25 Sep 2013
106	Tonga	15 January 2014
107	Lesotho	11 February 2014

ABOUT THE AUTHOR

LL.M. Spiro Paço is currently Director of the Department of Curricula and Quality Standards at "Aleksandër Moisiu" University, Durres, Albania. He has completed Bachelor studies in "Law" with very good results at "Luarasi" University College and "Master" (LL.M.) studies at the University of Greenwich in "International and Commercial Law".

Mr. Paço is a member of the National Chamber of Advocates in the Republic of Albania.

He has conducted various trainings in Albanian and EU Institutions on topics such as: Constitutional Law; EU and US institutions; Prevention of Money Laundering and Terrorism Financing; World history; geopolitical; Migration issues; Theoretical Issues on Governance Systems etc.

Mr. Paço is a participant in several scientific conferences at home and abroad and in many projects of academic character. He has been engaged as Lawyer (Head of Legal Office, Head of Human Resources Office, Counselor) at some of the most well-known companies in Albania. He's Academic Engagement has started at the University of Durrës "Aleksandër Moisiu", as a lecturer of "Institution History" and " Environment Law" courses.

For two years he has been a part of the academic staff of the Luarasi University College, at the Public Department and has given his contribution as lecturer in the courses of "History of Institutions", "History of Law in Albania", "Constitutional Law", "Philosophy and Law".

www.ingramcontent.com/pod-product-compliance
Lightning Source LLC
Chambersburg PA
CBHW030528220526
45463CB00007B/2757